A Family in Sri Lanka

LIBRARY OF CONGRESS CATALOGING IN PUBLICATION DATA

Bennett, Gay.
   A family in Sri Lanka.

   Rev. ed. of: Sri Lanka. 1980.
   Summary: Depicts life in a small village in Sri Lanka.
   1. Sri Lanka—Social life and customs—Juvenile
literature. [1. Sri Lanka—Social life and customs]
I. Cormack, Christopher, ill.   II. Bennett, Gay.
Sri Lanka.   III. Title.
DS489.15.B46   1985   954.9'3   85-6891
ISBN 0-8225-1661-6 (lib. bdg.)

Manufactured in the United States of America

2   3   4   5   6   7   8   9   10   95   94   93   92   91   90   89   88   87   86

A Family in Sri Lanka

Gay Bennett

Photographs by Christopher Cormack

Lerner Publications Company · Minneapolis

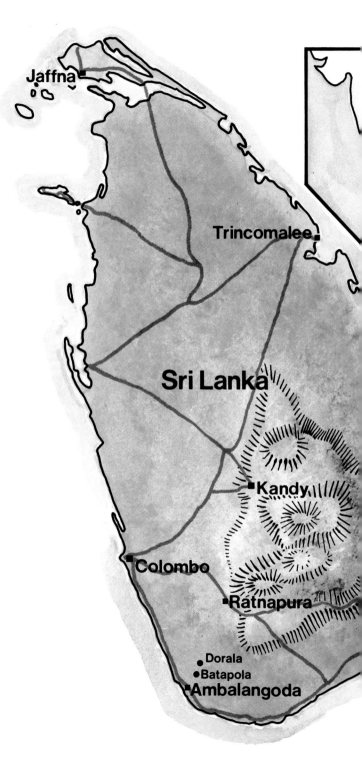

This is Nimal. He is 12 years old and lives in Dorala, a small village in the southern part of Sri Lanka (sree LAHNG kuh). Sri Lanka is an island off the southern tip of India.

Dorala is about 60 miles (100 kilometers) away from Colombo, the capital of Sri Lanka. To get from Colombo to Dorala, you must first take a bus. On the way, the bus stops at roadside stands so the passengers can get a drink of fresh coconut juice and a snack of curried prawns.

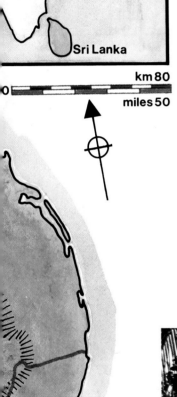

When the bus arrives in the village of Batapola, it stops. Those people going to Dorala must walk the rest of the way. The trail to Dorala is only a couple of miles long. It crosses green fields of rice and goes through tall coconut groves. It leads to the village shop.

Most of the houses in Dorala are hidden among the trees, away from the main path. Nimal's house was built by his father. It's surrounded by mango, banana, lime, coconut, orange, and cashew nut trees.

Nimal lives with his parents, his two brothers, Baba and
Nihal, and his grandmother. Every day at noon his father
comes home from the fields, and the family sits down to
lunch. Lunch is the main meal of the day. Nimal is always
late because he has to walk home from school in Batapola.

Baba is 7 years old and goes to school in Dorala. Nihal
is 18 and is finished with school. He helps their father
work on the land. Their grandmother helps their mother
with the cooking.

Almost every day, Nimal's grandmother cuts up pieces of jack fruit for lunch. Ripe jack fruit tastes like a mixture of banana and melon.

Unripe jack fruit is cooked like a vegetable and eaten as a curry, made with lots of different herbs and freshly ground spices.

Nimal's grandmother also takes care of the family's pet parrot, Pettha.

This is Nimal's mother. Every morning she gets up at 5:30 A.M. to prepare breakfast. She doesn't have any modern appliances or instant foods. Just to boil water for tea, she must first find some wood and then make a fire.

Nimal's house doesn't have running water. Each morning his mother goes down to the well at the bottom of the hill and carries up the water she will need to make breakfast.

Nimal's family shares two wells with four other families. The water from one well is used for cooking and drinking. The other well is used for washing. Every afternoon, Nimal's mother takes Baba there for a bath.

The family grows a lot of their own food. What they can't grow, they buy at the village store and at the weekly market in Batapola. The market has every kind of fruit, vegetable, and spice. It also sells fish, pots, pans, medicines, mirrors, and umbrellas. In Sri Lanka, people use umbrellas to protect themselves from the sun as well as from the rain.

When there are extra limes or oranges on his family's trees, Nimal takes them to the market after school and tries to sell them.

The village store is open every day. It sells coconut oil, used for cooking, and kerosene oil, used in lamps. In the corner of the store, a piece of rope is kept smoldering. People use it to light their cigarettes.

The only other shop in Dorala is the government store, where families collect their weekly ration of rice. The government gives this rice to families who cannot grow or buy all the food they need.

This rice isn't enough to feed Nimal's whole family, so his father grows more rice on a neighbor's land. In return for using the land, he gives the neighbor a quarter of the rice harvested.

Nimal's family eats rice and coconut at almost every meal. His father picks the coconuts himself. He ties a piece of rope between his ankles to help him grip the trunk of the palm and then shinnies up to the top of the tree.

The people of Sri Lanka use every part of the coconut. They drink the juice inside, grate the white part to eat, make bowls or spoons out of the shells, and dry the outer fiber. The fiber is twisted into mats or bags. They even use the leaves of the tree to make roofs on their houses.

In the village, Nimal's father is known as "the man with the cows." He owns two cows and one calf. The family drinks some of the cows' milk and sells the rest to neighbors.

When Nimal's father started to farm, he didn't own any land. The government lent him an acre and a half. Each year, Nimal's father pays a little more toward this land, and one day he will own it.

Nimal's father grows all the coconuts and jack fruit that the family eats. He also grows some cinnamon, which he sells. He makes a little extra money by working for the local landowners.

Farmers with a lot of land need help preparing the rice fields for the rainy season of April and May. Nimal's father works with three other men, turning over the earth so that it will absorb as much rain as possible. He uses a *mammoty*, a tool like a hoe.

Sri Lanka is famous for growing tea, but Dorala is in the region where most of the world's cinnamon is grown. It is used in curry, cakes, cookies, candy, and hot chocolate.

Peeling the cinnamon branches is Nimal's job. He usually works with two friends. Santha strips off the outer bark, and Nimal peels off the bright green inner bark, where the flavor is. Premalal rolls the peel into long sticks. They are dried, smoked, bundled together, and then sold all over the world.

No part of the cinnamon branch is wasted. The outer bark is used as fertilizer and the bare branches make good firewood. The leaves are taken to the village distillery, where they are steamed to produce cinnamon oil. This oil is bottled and sold to many countries.

Cinnamon oil is often added to medicines. When he has a toothache, Nimal's mother puts a drop of oil on his tooth. In the hill country, people rub cinnamon oil on their chests to ward off colds and chills.

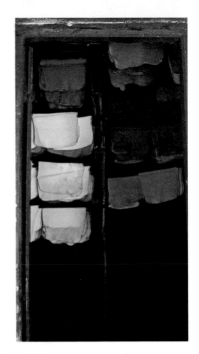

Nihal works on the local rubber estate whenever he is needed. Sometimes Nimal goes with him to help "tap" the trees. They make cuts in the bark of the rubber trees, and latex, a creamy white sap, oozes out. It runs into cups made from coconut shells.

After about two hours, they collect the latex in tin trays. It sets into sheets, which they stamp with the mark of the rubber estate. Later on the same day, they put the squares through a mangle to squeeze out any water and hang them out to dry.

The white squares of rubber are then smoked for five days. The squares turn yellow and become almost transparent. They are sold to manufacturers who turn them into all kinds of products, including car and bicycle tires.

In Dorala a bicycle is a family's most treasured possession. People live so far from the shops and schools—and from their neighbors—that without a bicycle they have to walk long distances every day.

Those villagers who don't own a bicycle sometimes rent one for the day or the week. They use it for errands, such as taking bundles of cinnamon sticks to local traders.

The bicycle shop is in Batapola. It is owned by Mr. De Silva, who rents, repairs, and sells bicycles. The sign in front of his shop is in Sinhalese. Three-fourths of the Sri Lankan people, including Nimal, speak Sinhalese. The sign gives the name of the road: *Siri Anoma Dassie Mawatha. Mawatha* means road or avenue.

New bicycles are very expensive, so Mr. De Silva and his sons try to repair all bicycles, even those over 30 years old.

When a bicycle cannot be repaired, Mr. De Silva turns the wheels into bobbins for winding cotton thread.

Almost every house in Dorala has a weaving loom. Everywhere you go, you can hear the "clak clak" of the wooden looms. The mothers work at home, and the young girls work together in small workshops. They make sarongs, the skirt-like garments worn by most men in Sri Lanka.

At first, the weaving industry brought more money to families in Dorala. But when stores in Sri Lanka began selling clothes from other countries more cheaply, fewer people bought homemade sarongs. Now there isn't enough work for everyone in the village.

The cotton thread for the sarongs comes from India. It's dyed different colors and dried in the sun. It takes many yards of cotton to make just one inch of sarong. Each sarong is over seven feet long, and most girls produce two a day.

The only other job open to young girls in Dorala is picking tea, but very little tea is grown here. Most is grown in the hill country.

One very important person in Dorala is Mr. Sirisena, the blacksmith. He makes and repairs tools, using any scrap metal he can find. It's a village joke that he can make anything out of anything.

Mr. Sirisena made Nimal's cinnamon peeling knife. He has made buckets, saucepans, coconut scrapers, and kettles for Nimal's mother.

Mr. Sirisena is 77 years old, but he still works at his anvil every day. His son and grandson help him.

The only tool that Mr. Sirisena doesn't make is the *mammoty*. The local steel isn't strong enough for all the hard work the *mammoty* has to do, so the blades must be ordered from England.

Nimal has a *mammoty*. He uses it at school when he and his classmates learn about growing crops.

After school, Nimal and his friends sometimes have a game of volleyball. They usually play in the early evening, when it's cool.

On Sundays, Nimal goes to the village temple. There the children learn about Lord Buddha. They are taught by Buddhist monks, who wear orange robes, and by some of the older children.

Buddha was a prince who lived a long time ago. Although he was very rich, he was troubled by the suffering of others. One day, he decided to leave his home and family to seek a way to ease life's suffering. He is said to have found the way while sitting under a shady bo tree, also called a bodhi tree. Bodhi means enlightenment, and Buddha means Enlightened One.

Statues of Buddha often show him sitting with his legs crossed in the lotus position.

At home, before the midday meal, Nimal's mother always lays an offering to Buddha in front of their small shrine. She gives Buddha a little rice, some water, and a few flowers.

In April, Buddhists celebrate Buddha's birthday with two days' holiday. Colored lights decorate the houses at night and the big towns have parades with elephants, fire-eaters, and dancers.

Nimal's family never goes on vacation because there's always too much work to do in the fields. Even when they take the bus to Ambalangoda to walk beside the sea or to see a movie, someone must stay at home to guard the cows.

One time, though, Nimal's father took him to Ratnapura, up in the hill country, to see the gem mines. Sri Lanka is famous for its jewels. Even in Dorala, people search for rubies, sapphires, and other gems in the stream.

The villagers sift the muddy water through a bamboo strainer and pick out any stones that catch their eye. So far, no one has found anything really valuable.

Nimal liked seeing the mines, but was glad to get home to his village, where everyone knows each other. His brother Nihal hopes to leave Dorala and get a job building houses in a large town. Nimal, though, wants to stay in Dorala when he grows up. He would like to become a teacher.

The History of Sri Lanka

Until 1972, Sri Lanka was called Ceylon. This tiny country has long been famous for growing tea and you may even have heard of Ceylon tea. Sri Lanka ranks third after two very large countries, India and China, in tea production.

The first people known to live on the island now called Sri Lanka were the Veddahs. They came from northern India in about 500 B.C. Some of these people stayed in the hill country of the island and are still called Veddahs today. But most of the descendents of these people form the group known as the Sinhalese. Like about three-fourths of all Sri Lankans, Nimal and his family are Sinhalese.

The next people to come to the island were the Tamils, who came from southern India. After that, small groups of people from Portugal, the Netherlands,Africa, Great Britain, and Malaysia all came to settle on the island.

For 150 years, Ceylon was a colony of Great Britain. The country achieved independence in 1948.

Facts about Sri Lanka

Capital: Colombo

Major Languages: Sinhala and Tamil

Form of Money: the rupee

Area: 25,332 square miles
(65,610 square kilometers)
  Sri Lanka is slightly larger than the state
  of West Virginia.

Population: about 15 million people
  There are more than 10 times as many
  people living in Sri Lanka than there are
  in West Virginia.

NORTH
AMERICA

SOUTH
AMERICA

EUROPE

A S I A

AFRICA

Sri Lanka

AUSTRALIA

Families the World Over

Some children in foreign countries live like you do. Others live very differently. In these books, you can meet children from all over the world. You'll learn about their games and schools, their families and friends, and what it's like to grow up in a faraway land.

Lerner Publications Company
241 First Avenue North
Minneapolis, Minnesota 55401